putting pare٫ting to bed

Study Guide

Putting Parenting to Bed: Study guide

© Ann Benton/The Good Book Company 2008

Reprinted 2010

Published by The Good Book Company

Elm House, 37 Elm Road, New Malden, Surrey KT3 3HB, UK

Tel (UK): 020-8942-0880

Tel (int): +(44) 208 942 0880

E-mail: admin@thegoodbook.co.uk

Websites:

UK & Europe: www.thegoodbook.co.uk

N America: www.thegoodbook.com

Australia: www.thegoodbook.com.au

New Zealand: www.thegoodbook.co.nz

ISBN: 9781905564897

Cover design by Carl Hamblin

Printed in India

CONTENTS

INTRODUCTION

1. What is the purpose of this course?

The course aims to help parents have the confidence to be parents. Parenting (in the sense of following theories, systems and programs for child-rearing) is a fairly new idea. It is now taken very seriously by many people—sometimes even by those who aren't actually doing it! In one way this is good: there is a sense in which raising our children is the most significant thing we do on this planet. In another way this is bad: it has turned parenting into something difficult and mysterious. We seem to forget that people have been successfully raising pleasant and civilised human beings for centuries! Most of those parents will never have read a single book on the subject, nor will they have attended a course. So how hard can it be?

We want to show that parents have within their grasp all that they need to do a decent job of raising children. There is heaps of advice available, but the course tries to keep things simple. It aims not to get too bogged down in fashionable "pop-psychology", but instead, to underline the basic principles which will give us a focus and direction in our parenting.

The basic principles are:

- **loving authority**
- **loving discipline**
- **loving relationship**

We hope that parents who are clear about these three things will be liberated to enjoy their children and the adventure of watching them develop and flourish.

2. What is it based on?

Anyone can say anything and back it up with statistics! However, this course is based on the wisdom of the Bible. The Bible is not a parenting manual; it is a book that claims to be from God and about God. It tells a huge story, which begins with the creation of the universe and ends, after a dramatic rescue involving the death and raising to life of God's own Son, with saved, forgiven people being welcomed into heaven.

But within the pages of the Bible, we find pointers to the best way to live. People from different times and places who have used these pointers as their guide in parenting have testified how sound, true and helpful this advice is for everybody, whatever their background or religion.

This course has probably been organised by your local church, and the leader (or leaders) will be Christians, who will be happy to help you with any questions or issues about the Christian faith that may arise during the course.

You will find that in each section of this *Study Guide* quotations from the Bible have been included to set you thinking.

3. Who is it for?

Putting Parenting to Bed will have something in it for any parent or parent-to-be. It doesn't really deal with nitty-gritty subjects (like how to toilet train a child—there are plenty of books with suggestions on that kind of thing). Instead, it focuses on principles which can be applied whether a child is three or thirteen. Obviously, those who are just starting their parenting adventure will have more opportunity to set their direction according to the principles laid down in the course. But on the other hand, it is still useful for those parents midway through the task to pause, evaluate and make changes.

4. What will happen at each session?

Putting Parenting to Bed will normally be held over three sessions, each of which will last about two hours (although it may also be run in six shorter sessions). It consists of a mix of listening and discussing, and watching short extracts from popular films, which will introduce the key concept for each session.

People learn in a variety of ways. Listening enables us to receive information. By using this *Study Guide* while you listen, and filling in gaps or noting down anything you find helpful in the spaces provided, you will be helping yourself to remember the things that you really want to take on board. You will also then be able to go home with a summary of what has been taught.

Some of us process information best by talking things through with others. So within each session there will be opportunities to discuss or answer questions in a small group.

Finally, there are questions to think over and answer at home between the sessions. If you have a husband/wife/partner, it is fairly important to talk through what you are learning; if possible, it would be even better to make arrangements so that you can attend the course together.

1: THE TROUBLE WITH PARENTING — PARENTS!

Key concept:
Loving authority

A. WHAT IS A CHILD?

Watch!
The film extract

Discuss!

1. *In the scene from the film, what are the parents doing?*

2. *Introduce your child/children to the people around you.*
Mention at least three good things about each of your children.

3. *Is there anything about your child/children which makes you think you might one day be called in for an interview at school?*

Presentation A: What is a child?

• *Circle any of the following answers with which you agree.*

• *Note down any consequences of thinking of a child in this way.*

1. a random collection of atoms/chemicals

2. uniquely created

3. a consumer item/fashion accessory

4. innocent

5. naturally wayward

6. a blank sheet of paper

7. genetically programmed

"For you created my inmost being; you knit me together in my mother's womb."

Psalm 139 v 13

"An arrow into the future"

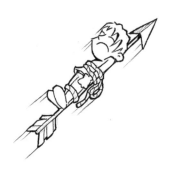

"Train up a child in the way he should go; even when he is old he will not depart from it." Proverbs 22 v 6

B. PARENTING PITFALLS

Discuss!

1. *What sort of parent are you?*

2. *Most of what we know about parenting we have learned from our own parents.*
Reflect on the way your parents brought you up. Think of some of the things they did for
you or to you. What standards did they set you?

Listen & Note

Presentation B: An alphabet of parenting pitfalls

These are some of the unhelpful habits that all of us, even as loving parents,
can get into while coping with our children.

Pitfall	Reason	Result	Antidote
A. Allow anything			

11

Pitfall	Reason	Result	Antidote
B. Bribery			
C. Child-centred			
D. Distant			
E. Explosive			
F. Fault-finding			
G. Guilty			

Pitfall	Reason	Result	Antidote
H. Hedging			
I. Inconsistent			

Discuss!

1. *"The trouble with parenting is that you can't get the staff." Is that true? Why?*

2. *Why do some parents have a problem with authority?*

3. *Raising a child requires more than authority? What else is important?*

1. How would you defend the idea that every child is precious?

2. In what sense are children both innocent and wayward?

3. Based on what you have learned so far, write a job description for a parent.

"A child left to himself disgraces his mother."
Proverbs 29 v 15

2: THE BIG D-WORD — DISCIPLINE!

Key concept:
Loving obedience

C. COMMUNICATION

Watch!

The film extract

Discuss!

In the extract from The Sound of Music, what was the problem...

1. *from the children's point of view?*

2. *from the Captain's point of view?*

Presentation C: Communication

STYLES OF PARENTING

- *What are the three styles of parenting?*
- *How do they affect the way we discipline (or don't discipline) our children?*
- *Underline the one that is closest to your style.*
- *Circle the best way of parenting.*

1.

2.

3.

> **Rules without relationship lead to rebellion**

THE "MAGIC TRIAD"

Join up the three elements of the "magic triad".

communication

discipline   **relationship**

EFFECTIVE COMMUNICATION

- *What four things are needed for effective communication?*

- *What can go wrong at each stage?*

1.

2.

3.

4.

"*Therefore encourage one another and build one another up.*" *1 Thessalonians 5 v 11*

D. DISCIPLINE

"Folly is bound up in the heart of a child."

Proverbs 22 v 15

Presentation D: Discipline

WHY DO CHILDREN MISBEHAVE?

Reason	Example	My strategy
To get attention		
To challenge authority		
To hurt		
To win a friend's approval		
To signal inadequacy		

THE PARENTS' RESPONSIBILITY

a) Expect obedience

Note down the six-point strategy for training in obedience.

1.

2.

3.

4.

5.

6.

b) Decide on your particular focus

- Establish focus

- Explain focus

- Enact focus

- Enforce focus

- Sanctions

    Use natural consequences eg:

    Use logical consequences eg:

    Use direct action eg:

"Honour your father and your mother."

Exodus 20 v 12

c) Turn a behaviour crisis into a learning opportunity.

Write out the 5 questions used in the training strategy.

1.

2.

3.

4.

5.

SUMMARY

Remember...

• The unrivalled partnership:

• The ultimate product:

• The unashamed propaganda:

"A refusal to correct is a refusal to love; love your children by disciplining them." Proverbs 13 v 24
("The Message" paraphrase of the Bible)

1. *Share with the group a typical example of child misbehaviour that you have witnessed. Which category or categories does it come under? How should that affect the parent's response?*

2. *Where have you noticed that "good children are happy children"?*

1. *How obedient is your child? Why is it in his/her interest to know that your word is law?*

2. *What behaviour focus do you think you should set for your child/children right now?*

3: LIVE AND INTERACTIVE!
—RELATIONSHIP!

Key concept:
Loving relationship

E. MYTHS AND MISTAKES

Watch!

The film extract

Discuss!

After watching the film extract, talk with others about how well you know your child.

See if you can answer these questions:

• *What did you give him/her last birthday?*

• *What is his/her favourite food?*

• *What does he/she like best at school?*

• *What worries your child?*

• *Where would he/she like to spend an ideal day out?*

Presentation E: Myths and Mistakes

1. The myth of quality time

- *What is wrong with it?*

- *What is the alternative?*

2. The myth of "educational"

- *What is wrong with it?*

- *What is the alternative?*

3. The myth of things

- *What is wrong with it?*

- *What is the alternative?*

1. *How much time do you spend "relating" to your children, rather than just being "around" them? What are some of the things you enjoy doing with them, just for enjoyment's sake?*

2. *How concerned are you about the things your children have? How concerned are they? If this is an area that you need to address, how will you go about it?*

Jesus said: "A man's life does not consist in the abundance of his possessions." Luke 12 v 15

F. VALUES AND VIRTUES

Discuss!

Imagine your child aged 21. What sort of a person do you want him/her to be?

Make a list of desirable qualities.

Listen & Note

Presentation F: Values and Virtues

1. EVALUATE THE INPUT

a) Your child is a receiver. What messages is he/she receiving?

b) Your child is a worshipper. What will be "Number1" in his or her life?

"Those who make idols will be like them, and so will all who trust in them." Psalm 115 v 8

2. BALANCE THE INPUT.

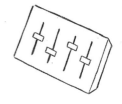

Four areas to keep in mind.

- **intellectual**

    which includes:

- **physical**

    which includes:

- **spiritual**

    which includes:

- **social/emotional**

    which includes:

3. CHECK OUT THE RESOURCES

"And Jesus grew in wisdom and stature, and in favour with God and men." Luke 2 v 52

1. **"Parenting is a burden."**

 - *In what ways do you find it so?*

 - *Who are you able to share this burden with?*

2. **"Parenting is exquisite."**

 - *What precious memories do you already have?*

 - *What experiences do you intend to share with your child?*

1. *What messages does your child receive inside the home and outside the home?*

2. *Assess your child's most pressing developmental needs currently in each of the four areas.*

- Intellectual

- Physical

- Social/Emotional

- Spiritual

- *How will you attempt to meet them? What resources will you make use of?*

3. *Which of the four areas are you most likely to neglect? What will you do about it?*

Aren't they lovely when they're asleep
Ann Benton (Christian Focus Publications)
ISBN: 9781857928761. 125pp.

Ann Benton used to run parenting skills classes in local schools. People kept saying "This is great, where do you get this stuff?" She came clean: "Actually, it's from the Bible." This book contains the wisdom distilled from Ann's popular seminars on parenting the next generation. She uses a "God's-eye view" of what we are really like, in order to help people who are seeking to be responsible parents in an increasingly child-centred society. You will learn six key concepts: accept, beware, communicate, discipline, evaluate and fear the Lord. These are applied with understanding and sensitivity.

Fatherhood
Tony Payne (Matthias Media)
ISBN: 9781876326999. 189pp.

"In the course of this book, I want to change your mind about fathering. I want to change the way you think about it, both consciously and instinctively. And if I succeed, it will change the way you act every day in a thousand ways. It will make you a better father." In this very readable book, Tony Payne takes a fresh look at what the Bible says about dads. What does it really mean to be a father? What should fathers be trying to achieve? And how can they do a better job? He answers these questions with insight, practical wisdom and good humour.

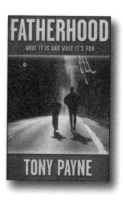

PUTTING PARENTING TO BED
Evaluation Form

Please complete and then detach this page from the book and give it to the leader of the course.

Please mark the appropriate boxes.

Which sessions have you attended?

☐ The trouble with parenting   ☐ The big D-word   ☐ Live and interactive

- *What was your rating of the course?*

	Poor	Satisfactory	Good
Content			
Style			
Timing			

- *What did you find most helpful?*

- *What did you / will you try to put into practice?*

- *Any further comments?*

- *Were you surprised to hear that the Bible contains guidance relevant for parenting today?*
  ☐ **Yes** ☐ **No**

- *Would you be interested in hearing more about the Christian faith?* ☐ **Yes** ☐ **No**

If you would be interested in attending a short course exploring the Christian faith, please write your contact details below.

Name: _____

Contact number: _____

Please use the back for any other comments you would like to add.
All information is treated with the strictest confidence.